Ben Franklin's Glass Armonica

Ben Franklin's Glass Armonica

by Bryna Stevens
pictures by Priscilla Kiedrowski

Carolrhoda Books • Minneapolis, Minnesota

Manufactured in the United States of America

LIBRARY OF CONGRESS CATALOGING IN PUBLICATION DATA

Stevens, Bryna.
  Ben Franklin's glass armonica.

  (A Carolrhoda on my own book)
  Summary: Describes the new musical instrument invented
by Ben Franklin for which Wolfgang Amadeus Mozart and
Ludwig van Beethoven composed music.
  1. Glass harmonica—Juvenile literature. 2. Franklin,
Benjamin, 1706-1790—Juvenile literature. [1. Glass
harmonica. 2. Franklin, Benjamin, 1706-1790] I. Kied-
rowski, Priscilla, ill. II. Title. III. Series.
ML3930.A2S84   1983   789'.6   82-9715
ISBN 0-87614-202-1

    1 2 3 4 5 6 7 8 9 10 92 91 90 89 88 87 86 85 84 83

to Mark, who always encouraged and inspired me
—B. Stevens

to John, for keeping my pencils sharp
—P. Kiedrowski

What do you think of when you hear the name Benjamin Franklin? The Declaration of Independence? Flying a kite in a thunderstorm? Many things come to mind, but music usually doesn't.

Actually Ben Franklin was a very fine musician. He knew how to play the harp, the guitar, and the violin. Once he even invented a new musical instrument. This is the story of that invention.

It all began in China. A clever
Chinese girl had an idea. She tapped
a glass with a stick.

"What a pretty sound," she said.

She filled the glass with water and
tapped it again. Now the sound was
lower.

Then she drank some of the water. She tapped the glass once more. The sound was higher.

The Chinese girl put a few glasses together. Each glass held a different amount of water. By tapping different glasses, she could play tunes.

All of her friends loved the glass music. So did some travelers who were in China. When the travelers went home to Europe, they told everyone about the Chinese girl's music. Soon people all over Europe were playing musical glasses.

One of those people was Edmund Delaval. Around 1761, he gave a musical-glass concert in London, England. Ben Franklin was staying in London at the time. He went to Delaval's concert.

Franklin loved music. He loved to play his harp, his guitar, and his violin. He especially liked to play Scotch folk songs, but sometimes he played music that he had written himself.

Franklin watched Delaval carefully. Delaval stood in front of several crystal glasses. Each glass held a different amount of water.

Mr. Delaval wet one of his fingers. He rubbed it around the rim of a glass. It made a clear, beautiful sound. Then he rubbed the rim of another glass. It made a different sound. Mr. Delaval played many songs on his crystal glasses.

Franklin liked the tunes that Delaval played.

"This music is so sweet and clear," he thought. "But Mr. Delaval plays so slowly. I like my music fast. Delaval can play only one note at a time. I like lots of notes played together. Chords and harmonies make music interesting."

The next day Franklin sat at his desk. He thought about the concert. Then he drew something on a piece of paper.

"I think I can improve the musical glasses," he said.

Franklin ran outside. He called for a hansom cab.

"Take me to Charles James's," he said to the driver. "He lives on Purpool Lane."

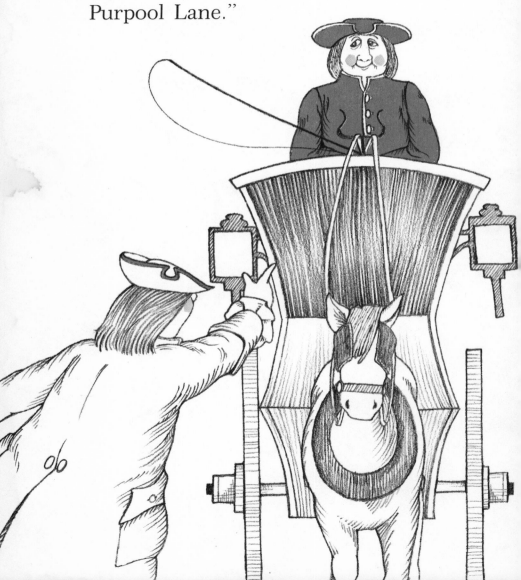

Franklin entered Charles James's glass shop. James was making a bowl.

"I want to order 37 glass bowls," Franklin said to James. "Each bowl must have a hole in its center."

"Holes in their centers?" said Charles James. "Then the bowls will leak."

"It doesn't matter," said Franklin. "The bowls are not for holding anything. They are for playing music."

Charles James was puzzled, but all he said was, "Oh." He didn't want to question the famous Dr. Franklin.

When the bowls were ready, Franklin tuned them. He wanted each one to sound like a musical note. When a bowl didn't sound right, he ground off some glass. When he finished, each bowl sounded like a different note. Then he painted their rims different colors.

"Colors will make each note easier to pick out," he said.

He painted all the Cs red. He painted all the Ds orange. All the Es were yellow. All the Fs were green. He painted the Gs blue. The As were dark blue. The Bs were purple.

He painted some bowls white. The white bowls sounded like the black keys on a modern piano.

Franklin laid all the bowls on their sides. He arranged them from the largest bowl to the smallest. Then he ran a long iron rod through their centers. He attached the rod to a wheel. The wheel was attached to a foot pedal.

Franklin pressed the foot pedal.

The rod began to turn. The bowls began to spin. So far, everything was working.

Franklin sat down at his instrument. He kept the bowls spinning. He wet his fingers. Then he rubbed them with chalk. The chalk would help "catch" the glass.

Franklin touched the rim of a bowl. What a beautiful sound it made! Then he touched another and another. Soon Franklin could play tunes with one hand. He played chords and harmonies with the other hand.

Franklin loved his instrument.
The music was sweet and clear.
He called it an *armonica*. Armonica
means "harmony" in Italian. But
many people came to call it Franklin's glass harmonica.

Franklin's armonica was the first instrument invented by an American. He built a small carrying case for it, and he often carried it with him while he was in Europe.

When people asked him to play, he usually did. Sometimes he played his favorite Scotch folk songs. Sometimes he played songs that he had written himself. Franklin loved to play the glass armonica!

Finally it was time for Ben Franklin to leave Europe. He was going home to Philadelphia. The trip was a long one. It took about 41 days to cross the Atlantic Ocean in those days.

At last Franklin got home. It was very late at night when he arrived. Mrs. Franklin was sleeping. Ben didn't want to wake her up. He was tired too, but he wanted to relax with some music before he went to bed.

Franklin tiptoed to the attic. He carried his armonica with him. He put it together and played some songs.

The sweet sound of the music drifted downstairs. Mrs. Franklin stirred. She was only half awake. When she heard the music, she thought she was dead. She thought the music was angels singing. She thought she had died and gone to heaven.

Franklin's armonica became very popular. A newspaper in Germany said it was a great invention. George Washington wrote about it in his diary. Thomas Jefferson said it made the greatest music of the century. Wolfgang Amadeus Mozart and Ludwig van Beethoven, two famous composers, liked the armonica too. They both wrote music for it. Even the Queen of France, Marie Antoinette, took armonica lessons.

One of the most popular armonica players was Marianne Kirchgessner. She was a blind musician, and she played the armonica very well. She gave many concerts. Everyone liked to hear her play.

But one day she got very sick. Pressing her fingers against the vibrating glass bowls had damaged her nerves. Her armonica career was over.

Other armonica players had the same problem. Playing the armonica made them sick. So some inventors tried to improve Franklin's instrument.

Leopold Rollig built a keyboard. Players touched keys on the keyboard instead of glass bowls. But Rollig's keyboard armonica didn't sound very good.

P. J. Frick placed pads between the bowls. The glass bowls didn't vibrate as much then. They were less likely to make players sick. But an armonica with pads didn't sound very pretty either.

One man tried to play the armonica with two violin bows. But the bows were hard to handle. This wasn't a good solution either.

No one could improve Franklin's glass armonica. Nothing sounded as fine as fingers pressing on the glass bowls. But that was exactly what was making the players sick.

Many people became afraid of the armonica. Some thought it had magical powers. Some said it revived people who had fainted. Others claimed it made people faint. One man said the armonica made his dog chase its tail. A doctor claimed the armonica cured thickness of the blood.

A man in Germany said the armonica had killed his child. He called the police. The police became frightened. They banned the armonica in some German towns.

People grew more and more afraid of the armonica. Soon they stopped playing it altogether. Franklin, though, kept right on. The armonica never made him sick at all.

Most people forgot all about the glass armonica until 1956—Franklin's 250th birthday. Franklin, of course, had died long before then. But people in Boston, Massachusetts, wanted to celebrate his birthday any-

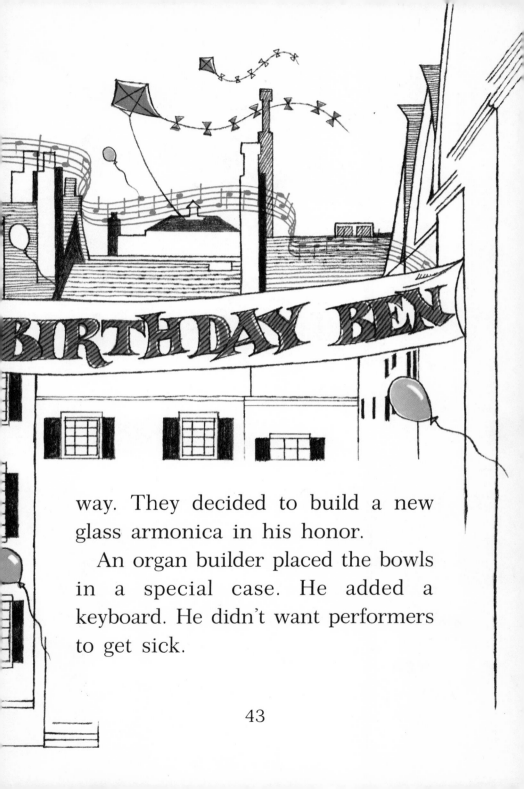

way. They decided to build a new glass armonica in his honor.

An organ builder placed the bowls in a special case. He added a keyboard. He didn't want performers to get sick.

E. Power Biggs, a world-famous
organist, played the new armonica
in a concert. People loved it. They
enjoyed hearing Mozart's music for
glass armonica. They also enjoyed
hearing the music that Benjamin
Franklin had written himself.

Records of Mozart's music for glass armonica have been made, but there aren't very many real glass armonicas left any more. Performers now play glass armonica music on electronic instruments. Electronic instruments ·don't break as easily as glass bowls, and they don't make their players sick. But they will probably never sound as beautiful as Ben Franklin's glass armonica!

About the Author

Bryna Stevens has always loved music. She graduated from Music and Art High School in New York City and received a degree in music from the University of Wisconsin. Ms. Stevens has given piano lessons, directed choirs, and taught music to handicapped children. Nor is she a newcomer to the field of writing. She is the author of several books and numerous articles. Ms. Stevens is currently living in Greensboro, North Carolina.

About the Artist

Priscilla Kiedrowski grew up in Richfield, Minnesota, and attended the College of Art and Design and Hennepin Technical Center, both in Minneapolis. She now works as a commercial artist. Ms. Kiedrowski lives in Maple Grove, Minnesota, with her 14-year-old son, John. This is her first book.